2

Faith & Facts

Participant's Guide

Other Resources by Lee Strobel

The Case for Christ
The Case for Christ audio
The Case for Christ—Student Edition (with Jane Vogel)
The Case for Christmas
The Case for a Creator
The Case for a Creator audio
The Case for Creator—Student Edition (with Jane Vogel)
The Case for Easter
The Case for Faith
The Case for Faith audio
The Case for Faith—Student Edition (with Jane Vogel)
Experiencing the Passion of Jesus (with Garry Poole)
God's Outrageous Claims
Inside the Mind of Unchurched Harry and Mary
Surviving a Spiritual Mismatch in Marriage
    (with Leslie Strobel)
Surviving a Spiritual Mismatch in Marriage audio
What Jesus Would Say

Other Resources by Garry Poole

The Complete Book of Questions
Seeker Small Groups
The Three Habits of Highly Contagious Christians

In the Tough Questions Series:

Don't All Religions Lead to God?
How Could God Allow Suffering and Evil?
How Does Anyone Know God Exists?
Why Become a Christian?
Tough Questions Leader's Guide (with Judson Poling)

2

Faith & Jesus

Participant's Guide

Four Sessions on the Bible, Heaven, Hell, and Science

Lee Strobel and Garry Poole

ZONDERVAN™

GRAND RAPIDS, MICHIGAN 49530 USA

WILLOW

Willow Creek Resources

ZONDERVAN.COM/
AUTHORTRACKER

ZONDERVAN™

Faith & Facts Participant's Guide
Copyright © 2006 by Lee Strobel and Rocket Pictures
Requests for information should be addressed to:
Zondervan, *Grand Rapids, Michigan 49530*

ISBN-10: 0-310-26851-6

ISBN-13: 978-0-310-26851-2

All Scripture quotations, unless otherwise indicated, are taken from the *Holy Bible: New International Version®*. NIV®. Copyright © 1973, 1978, 1984 by International Bible Society. Used by permission of Zondervan. All rights reserved.

The website addresses recommended throughout this book are offered as a resource to you. These websites are not intended in any way to be or imply an endorsement on the part of Zondervan, nor do we vouch for their content for the life of this book.

Interior design by Angela Moulter

Printed in the United States of America

06 07 08 09 10 11 12 • 10 9 8 7 6 5 4 3 2 1

Contents

Special thanks to Ann Kroeker and Laura Allen for their outstanding writing and editing contributions. Their creative insights and suggestions took these guides to the next level.

Preface

The idea came to me in the shower one morning: why not create a television program in which people of various beliefs — from Muslims to Christians to atheists to New Agers — could debate the most provocative spiritual and moral issues of the day?

What's more, prominent religious leaders could be invited on the program to be cross-examined about the stickiest questions concerning their faith.

Thanks to the vision and creativity of Jim Berger and Joni Holder, we ended up producing *Faith Under Fire*™ for a national television network. As predicted, the weekly show generated a slew of vociferous letters from viewers around the country. More than one person admitted that he found himself shouting back at his TV set.

This curriculum is based on the interviews and debates we aired on the program. You'll see knowledgeable and passionate experts discussing not just *what* they believe, but *why* they believe it. Our hope is that your group will provide a safe environment for you to be able to share your own thoughts and opinions — as well as to consider the viewpoints of others.

You'll quickly see that many of the claims made by the experts are mutually exclusive. In other words, the Christian and Muslim cannot both be right if the Bible claims Jesus is the Son of God and the Koran asserts that he's not divine but merely a prophet. One of them might be correct, or both of them could be in error, but each one of them cannot be true at the same time.

That's why we insist that our experts back up their claims. Can they defend their position logically? Do they have evidence from history or science that supports their assertions? Our task should be to determine where the evidence points.

In a similar way, the U.S. Constitution provides equal protection to all expressions of faith, and yet that doesn't mean all religious claims are equally true. According to the U.S. Supreme Court, the American ideal is to create a "marketplace of ideas" in which various opinions and beliefs can freely battle with each other so that truth will ultimately prevail.

So what is "true" about God, about Jesus, and about the afterlife? What can we know with confidence about issues of faith and morality? I hope you'll grapple with these issues in unhindered debate and discussion in your group.

One thing is true for sure: a lot hinges on the outcome.

Lee Strobel

SESSION
1

Is the
Bible Bogus?

Read It!

Holy Smoke?

Eric and Heather, a young couple in their twenties, came to the discussion group because their neighbor Ted invited them. Ben and Elise get babysitting every week and ride their bikes a few minutes through the neighborhood to attend. Carol, a soft-spoken woman in her thirties, usually doesn't say much. She prefers to listen. "I'm just learning from you all," she frequently says. Nick and Heather keep things lively with their strong ideas about nearly every topic they've covered, and Peter facilitates the discussions to cover a variety of spiritual topics.

Last week, when they were discussing miracles, Nick threw out a challenge. "Peter," he said, "you're always using Bible verses for us to respond to, but I think the Bible is a pretty lousy resource book. Can we leave the Bible out of it?"

"I agree," said Ted, nodding.

"Me too," Heather said. In fact, everyone seemed intensely interested in this issue.

"That's a good point," Peter agreed. "Would you like to discuss the credibility of the Bible next week?" Everyone agreed. "Okay, then. Come ready to bring your issues and questions about whether or not the Bible can be trusted."

"That shouldn't be a problem," Nick said. "It won't take me any prep time at all. I can tell you right here and now everything that bugs me."

Peter laughed. "That's great—at least we're guaranteed an energetic start to our discussion!"

When they gathered the next week, Nick started. "Listen, I've read the Bible from cover to cover in five and a half months, and it's a very scary book."

"Tell me more," Peter urged.

"Don't get him started!" Ted exclaimed.

Nick grinned. "Ted and I have had some conversations about this over coffee. Okay, for one thing, the Bible is full of disturbing contradictions. It says, 'Thou shall not kill,' yet the Israelites said that God told them to wipe out an entire group of people. So you tell me how that can translate into a clear set of principles for me to follow!"

Eric jumped in. "Personally, I think that the Bible has some truth to it, but it's also full of errors ... the trick is figuring out which part is which."

"Well, that brings up something I wanted to point out," Ted interjected. "I think the Bible was written by humans, but Christians try to tell us that it's written by God. Then they turn right around and use it to manipulate and justify hurting people in the name of God. I hate that. I think it was written by people, and that it's totally impossible for a group of imperfect people to write a completely perfect book. The Bible may have some remarkable wisdom here and there, but it didn't come from God. It is a mixture of human truth and error."

"Good point," Nick affirmed. "I agree with that."

"I wonder why people think the Bible is better than any other holy book," Heather proposed. "There are so many sacred writings; shouldn't we treat them all with the same degree of respect and care?"

"Whoa, slow down!" Peter exclaimed. He was scribbling notes on a piece of paper. "You've brought up so many great points. Should we stop and discuss any of them in detail? I'm trying to keep up."

"No, I think we should get it all out on the table and then deal with them one by one," Nick stated. "So, Peter, here's another one for you to add to your list: People need to read the Bible critically, and I just don't see Christians doing that. They're so gullible."

"Well, where I come from, as a Buddhist, I was forbidden to read the Bible," Elise explained. "It's considered to be an evil book. But now that we've been referencing it in our group discussions, I've gotten to where I want to read it for myself to see if there's any truth to that."

"Don't bother," Nick said. "I just read it, and trust me: It's evil."

"Do you mean that?" Carol said. Everyone turned their attention to her. "Do you really and truly think it's evil, Nick?"

"Well, yeah, pretty much," he answered.

"Why do you ask, Carol?" Peter asked.

Carol stopped fiddling with the fringe of a pillow. "Well, I've been listening to all of you, and I love your ideas. I think you've brought up some great points, but I have to say one thing about the Bible. I've never thought it was evil, but I did think it was outdated and irrelevant. But then, like you, Nick, I decided to read it in the past few months, and it blew my mind. It's nothing like what I thought it was. It's as relevant as any self-help, philosophy, or religious book written today."

There was a pause in the flow of conversation. Carol rarely speaks her mind this firmly. "Thanks for sharing your opinion, Carol," Peter finally said, breaking the silence.

"Yeah," Nick said. "We're all entitled to our point of view."

Eric said, "Have you noticed that people interpret different passages all different ways? Who do we believe? Anyone can make the Bible say whatever they want, so how do we know what the authors of the Bible really intended to say?"

"Good question," Nick agreed. "A very good question."

Heather looked up. "Yeah, how do we know for sure *what* the Bible says?"

Watch It!

Use the following space to take notes as you view the video in which Lee Strobel interviews Dr. Michael Shermer, founding publisher of *Skeptic* magazine and author of several books, including *How We Believe*, and Dr. Ben Witherington III, a New Testament scholar at Asbury Seminary and the author of more than twenty books and commentaries, including the award-winning *The Jesus Quest*.

Discuss It!

1 Name a book you have recently read and would recommend to others. What did you like about it? What do you think are the top bestselling books of all time? Where does the Bible rank on your list?

2 Growing up, what do you remember hearing or believing about the Bible? Were you an "easy sell" or were you convinced the Bible was "bogus"? Explain your answer. How has your view of the Bible changed over the years?

3 Which of the following statements best describe your current view of the Bible?

- ❑ The Bible should be accepted as true by faith and without reservation.
- ❑ The Bible must be substantiated with convincing evidence.
- ❑ The Bible is filled with lots of contradictions.
- ❑ The Bible is outdated and irrelevant.
- ❑ The Bible should be scrutinized, but ultimately we must accept that there are some things about the Bible that we will never fully understand.

❑   The Bible has a lot of wisdom but that doesn't mean it's from God.

❑   The Bible is a mixture of truth and human error.

> "What I'm saying is, if God wanted to send us a message, and ancient writings were the only way he could think of doing it, he could have done a better job."
>
> **Dr. Arroway in Carl Sagan's *Contact***

4 Do you believe the Gospels are reliable or do they report mostly what the authors and others merely wish was true? Explain.

5 Michael Shermer is convinced the Bible is "myth history," and Ben Witherington says the ancient Jews were not myth-making people but intended to report only what had actually occurred. Based on what you've read of the Gospels, who do you think is right? Why?

> "Above all, you must understand that no prophecy of Scripture came about by the prophet's own interpretation. For prophecy never had its origin in the will of man, but men spoke from God as they were carried along by the Holy Spirit."
>
> **2 Peter 1:20–21**

6 Shermer argues that the Bible cannot be used to prove itself and that outside sources must be examined. Give reasons why you agree or disagree with him.

7 Which of the following four types of evidence—eyewitness accounts, numerous ancient manuscripts, archaeological findings, accurate prophetic predictions—if substantiated, would be the most compelling arguments for the credibility of the Bible? Why?

Watch It!

Use the following space for notes as Lee Strobel continues to interview Dr. Michael Shermer and Dr. Ben Witherington III.

Discuss It!

8 What specific errors, contradictions, or inaccuracies have you found in the Bible?

9 Shermer shares that he does not believe in such things as the paranormal or the supernatural, only in the normal and natural. What about you? What do you believe about the supernatural? Give reasons for your response. Do you think it's more reasonable to (1) rule out the possibility of the supernatural at the outset, or (2) follow the evidence of science and history wherever they lead, even if they point toward the existence of the supernatural? Why?

"I've made a hobby of collecting alleged discrepancies, inaccuracies, and conflicting statements in the Bible. I have a list of about eight hundred of them. A few years ago I coauthored a book called *When Critics Ask,* which devotes nearly six hundred pages to setting the record straight. All I can tell you is that in my experience when critics raise these objections, they invariably violate one of seventeen principles for interpreting Scripture."

Norman Geisler, PhD

10 To what extent do you believe that God has communicated to human beings through the Bible? Explain your response. What might be some possible obstacles to such a feat?

Inspiration of the Bible

Christians don't believe God literally dictated the Bible's contents. However, they do believe that the Bible contains the inspired Word of God.

Here's how biblical scholar Charles C. Ryrie explained it: "Inspiration is ... God's superintendence of the human authors so that, using their own individual personalities, they composed and recorded without error his revelation to man in the words of the original autographs."

Ryrie said that the Bible "tells the truth. Truth can and does include approximations, free quotations, language of appearances, and different accounts of the same event as long as those do not contradict."

11 Charles Ryrie believes the Bible "tells the truth." What does he mean by this statement? Do you agree with it? Why or why not?

12 Share your responses to the following:

- Something that surprises me about the Bible that I didn't really realize before this discussion is:

- A new question I have about the Bible that this discussion has surfaced is:

- Something that remains troublesome to me about the Bible is:

> "All Scripture is God-breathed and is useful for teaching, rebuking, correcting and training in righteousness, so that the man of God may be thoroughly equipped for every good work."
>
> **2 Timothy 3:16–17**

13 What would it take for you to place confidence in the Bible as truth from God and as the supreme guide for your life?

14 What practical difference would it make in your everyday experience to believe that the Bible is God's Word?

Watch It! *Lee's Perspective*

For years, I was a skeptic about the Bible—not because I had thoroughly studied it and concluded it was unreliable, but because I had heard enough snippets of criticism through the years to poison my view of the book. It wasn't until I analyzed the Bible thoroughly that I concluded it must have a divine origin.

Not only is its wisdom—particularly expressed in the Proverbs, the Psalms, and Jesus' teachings—breathtaking in its beauty and depth, but the Bible is based on key eyewitness accounts; it has been repeatedly corroborated by archaeological discoveries; it has specific predictions that were made hundreds of years in advance and that were literally fulfilled against all mathematical odds; and it contains credible and well-documented miracles that confirm its message. The New Testament's historical reliability, as I describe in my book *The Case for Christ*, is especially well-established, and the unprecedented proliferation of ancient manuscripts provides confidence that the Bible was accurately transmitted to us over the centuries.

So let me ask this: Do you know of any other book that matches its credentials?

Chart It!

At this point in your spiritual journey, what do you believe about the Bible? On a scale from one to ten, place an X near the spot and phrase that best describes you. Share your selection with the rest of the group and give reasons for placing your X where you did.

1	2	3	4	5	6	7	8	9	10
I'm not convinced the whole Bible is from God.				I'm unsure what to believe about the Bible.				I'm convinced the Bible — all of it — is God's Word.	

Study It!

Take some time later this week to check out what the Bible teaches about the reliability of its Scriptures.

+ Psalm 18:30
+ Psalm 33:4
+ Psalm 119
+ 2 Timothy 3:16
+ Hebrews 4:12
+ 2 Peter 1:20–21

SESSION
2

Is
Heaven Real?

Read It!

Who Knows?

An old family friend leaned forward and gave me a big hug. "Well, we all know he's in a better place," she whispered in my bad ear.

The next person shook my hand and smiled. "At least he's not suffering anymore."

A friend from church patted my shoulder and, with eyebrows raised hopefully, said, "He's up there celebrating right now, maybe even dancing, don't you think? That's right, he's dancing in heaven right now."

But I don't know what to think. Six months ago my father passed away. He had a long, hard battle with Parkinson's, and the funeral was packed with friends paying their respects. I know they meant well. They sincerely tried to comfort me, but really, what do they know?

The highly respected pastor spoke with great energy and conviction at the funeral service, "He's in a different venue, he's moved to a different location, he has a new home. His new home is now in heaven."

That was the climax of his message, the news that was supposed to give us hope: Dad's in heaven.

But what does he know? I mean, really, how does that pastor *know* that there's this place called heaven? He hasn't *been* there—in fact, as far as I know, no one has totally made it there and back, so how does anyone *really* know?

And what is heaven, anyway? Is it an actual location we'll float up to, complete with pearly gates and streets of gold and angels wafting around strumming harps? I hope not. Dad will be bored. He'll be trying to tell jokes or perform magic tricks with whatever deck of cards or coins he can find up there. Of course, they might not like magic tricks in heaven. But what do I know?

Will there really be no suffering, tears, or fears? No pain, disappointment, or Parkinson's? No poverty, starvation, or genocide? It would be nice if there really were a place like that. I hope there is.

But what if there isn't?

Maybe it's a parallel universe or a new existence so totally different from life on earth that there's nothing in our language to describe it. Maybe we just get sucked into some massive energy force. Maybe our soul or our spirit hurtles into a black hole and gets crushed to nothingness.

Maybe this life is it. Maybe this is all we get, and after that it's just *lights out*; worm food.

Or worse yet, what if there *is* a place called heaven ... and Dad's *not* there?

Or what if he's there and when it's my turn, *I'm* not welcome there?

What if we're both there, but we don't recognize each other?

All of that sounds more like hell than heaven.

Not long ago I decided to be candid about these thoughts with a friend. "How refreshing," he said. "It's refreshing to hear you admit your doubts because your struggle is so real."

Well, I'm sorry to say these questions aren't refreshing. Maybe my friend thinks they are because he's relating to them theoretically, but I just said good-bye to my dad. For me, these doubts are frustrating and discouraging. I might even go so far as to say *depressing*.

Bottom line, it feels like we're all grasping for something that we can never understand in this life as we know it. We don't *know* what's next. I'd love to know for sure. It would make things a little easier to deal with after losing my dad.

I want answers, but maybe there just aren't any.

Watch It!

Use the following space to take notes as you view the video in which Lee Strobel interviews bestselling author Randy Alcorn, founder of Eternal Perspective Ministries and author of the book *Heaven*.

"I would love to believe that when I die I will live again, that some thinking, feeling, remembering part of me will continue. But as much as I want to believe that, and despite the ancient and worldwide cultural traditions that assert an afterlife, I know of nothing to suggest that it is more than wishful thinking."

Carl Sagan

Discuss It!

1 When you picture heaven, what images come to mind? What is the basis for your ideas about heaven? How have your opinions changed over time?

2 Do you believe heaven is real? Why or why not? How certain are you of your belief?

"It goes on all day long and every day, during a stretch of twelve hours. The singing is of hymns alone, nay; it is of one hymn alone. The words are always the same; in number they are only about a dozen; there is no rhyme, there is no poetry."

Mark Twain, on music in heaven

3 Some atheists believe Christians made up the idea of heaven because they fear the finality of death. Do you think that's a viable criticism? Why or why not?

4 Which of the items listed below describe concerns or questions you've had as you've thought about heaven?

- ❏ Will it be boring?
- ❏ Is it just wishful thinking—does it even exist?
- ❏ Will we be able to recognize people?
- ❏ Will it be sad if every loved one isn't there?
- ❏ Will we become angels with halos and wings?
- ❏ Isn't eternity a long time to be at the same place?
- ❏ Other questions or concerns:

5 What evidence do you think supports the existence of heaven?

6 The reason Randy Alcorn says he's sure heaven exists is because Jesus, who also claimed to be the unique Son of God, *said* heaven exists. He explains that "if we believe Jesus, we believe what he says about heaven." How much weight do you give this argument? Why?

7 What do you think Alcorn means when he says, "There will be no self-righteous people in heaven, only people who have the *'righteousness of Christ'*"?

8 Read the Bible verses listed below. What do you think it means to be "righteous" in God's eyes? Where does this righteousness come from? Where does it not come from?

> What shall we conclude then? Are we any better? Not at all! We have already made the charge that Jews and Gentiles alike are all under sin. As it is written: "There is no one righteous, not even one; there is no one who understands, no one who seeks God. All have turned away." (Romans 3:9 – 12)

> I consider everything a loss compared to the surpassing greatness of knowing Christ Jesus my Lord ... that I may gain Christ and be found in him, not having a righteousness of my own that comes from the law, but that which is through faith in Christ — the righteousness that comes from God and is by faith. (Philippians 3:8 – 9)

> But when the kindness and love of God our Savior appeared, he saved us, not because of righteous things we had done, but because of his mercy. (Titus 3:4 – 5)

> God made him who had no sin to be sin for us, so that in him we might become the righteousness of God. (2 Corinthians 5:21)

Watch It!

Use the following space to take notes as Lee Strobel continues to interview Randy Alcorn.

Discuss It!

9 Randy Alcorn claims that people do not become angels in heaven and there is no marriage in heaven. What is your reaction to these two assertions? Are you surprised? Disappointed? Relieved? Explain.

10 If heaven is being with God, as Alcorn states, then what do you think it would be like to encounter God in heaven?

"[Beauty and joy on earth represent] only the scent of a flower we have not found, the echo of a tune we have not heard, news from a country we have never yet visited."

C. S. Lewis

> "The city does not need the sun or the moon to shine on it, for the glory of God gives it light.... The nations will walk by its light.... Nothing impure will ever enter it, nor will anyone who does what is shameful or deceitful, but only those whose names are written in the Lamb's book of life."
>
> **Revelation 21:23 – 24, 27**

11 Alcorn believes that "wherever God is, there is good, but where God is not, there is no good. Since hell is the one place where God will withdraw his presence, there will not be any fun or joy in hell. In fact, hell is a dark, lonely place." Do you agree with Alcorn's logic? Why or why not?

12 What do you think determines who goes to heaven and who does not? How confident are you that you will spend eternity in heaven? What is the basis for your level of confidence? What do you think of what the Bible says in Ephesians 2:8 – 9: "For it is by grace you have been saved, through faith — and this is not from yourselves, it is the gift of God — not by works, so that no one can boast."

Watch It! *Lee's Perspective*

In 2005, *Newsweek* relied on an anonymous source to claim that U.S. military interrogators had flushed the Koran down a toilet in order to compel Muslim prisoners to cooperate. The story sparked riots in the Middle East, resulting in more than a dozen deaths. But in a stunning reversal, *Newsweek* later conceded its source was faulty and apologized for its error. It was the most dramatic example in recent history of how important it is for journalists to rely only on highly credible sources of information.

That's why I think Randy Alcorn is right: when Jesus of Nazareth teaches about the reality of heaven, we can believe him. After all, he has established by his resurrection from the dead—a miraculous event that's well attested by the historical evidence—that he is the unique Son of God. And that puts him in a special position of having highly accurate information about what heaven is like.

When I was an atheist, I was willing to accept the finality of death. I certainly wasn't going to indulge in wishful thinking about heaven just because I was afraid of the end of life. But I'm grateful that there's credible evidence from a reliable source that the afterlife is real—and that access to heaven is available to anyone who chooses to receive Jesus' freely offered gift of forgiveness and grace.

Chart It!

At this point in your spiritual journey, what do you believe about heaven? On a scale from one to ten, place an X near the spot and phrase that best describes you. Share your selection with the rest of the group and give reasons for placing your X where you did.

1	2	3	4	5	6	7	8	9	10
I'm not convinced heaven exists.				I'm unsure what to believe about heaven.				I'm convinced heaven exists.	

Study It!

Take some time later this week to check out what the Bible teaches about heaven and life after death.

- ✦ Isaiah 66:1–2
- ✦ Matthew 6:19–21
- ✦ Matthew 8:5–13
- ✦ John 14:1–6
- ✦ Revelation 7:16–17

SESSION
3

Hell:
Fact or Fiction?

Read It!

Angry God?

O sinner! Consider the fearful danger you are in: it is a great furnace of wrath, a wide and bottomless pit, full of the fire of wrath, that you are held over in the hand of that God, whose wrath is provoked and incensed as much against you, as against many of the damned in hell.

The long-faced, serious preacher stood tall and slender in the pulpit on this particularly hot summer Sunday morning in 1741.

You hang by a slender thread, with the flames of divine wrath flashing about it, and ready every moment to singe it, and burn it asunder; and you have no interest in any Mediator, and nothing to lay hold of to save yourself, nothing to keep off the flames of wrath, nothing of your own, nothing that you ever have done, nothing that you can do, to induce God to spare you one moment.

He spoke slowly and somberly, almost methodically.

You are held in the hand of God, over the pit of hell; you have deserved the fiery pit, and are already sentenced to it.

The preacher filled his sermon with bold, descriptive statements about the realities of hell. But he delivered his words in an even tone, reading his notes most of the time—rarely looking up to make eye contact with the congregation.

There is nothing that keeps the wicked at any one moment out of hell, but the mere pleasure of God.

The small church in Enfield, Connecticut, was packed to overflowing. As if in a trance, they listened intently.

If God should let you go you would immediately sink and swiftly descend and plunge into the bottomless gulf, and your healthy constitution, and your own care and prudence, and best contrivance, and all your righteousness, would have no more influence to uphold you and keep you out of hell, than a spider's web would have to stop a falling rock.

No one walked out, no one looked away, no one moved. At first, the congregation was struck with shock and silence, hanging on every word and flinching with each blow. But then, slowly, the full impact of what they were hearing sank in. They began to weep, swoon, roll on the floor, and cry out as he spoke.

The God that holds you over the pit of hell, much as one holds a spider or some loathsome insect over the fire, abhors you, and is dreadfully provoked.

Yet he wasn't employing the typical hellfire and brimstone style. He was neither quick nor slow of speech and used no gestures to punctuate his points. His posture was still; he simply stood there, bracing an elbow against the pulpit with his notes in one hand. With well-placed pauses and distinct pronunciation, his calm, unemotional delivery gripped his listeners.

His wrath towards you burns like fire; he looks upon you as worthy of nothing else, but to be cast into the fire; he is of purer eyes than to bear to have you in his sight; you are ten thousand times more abominable in his eyes, than the most hateful venomous serpent is in ours.

The fear was palpable: Some men and women claimed that they could actually feel and even smell the flames of hell rising to the seats where they sat. Hell had become so real to these New Englanders that at one point in the sermon, the cries of the people drowned out the preacher and he had to pause for some time before continuing.

That world of misery, that lake of burning brimstone ... the dreadful pit of the glowing flames of the wrath of God; there is hell's wide gaping mouth open; and you have nothing to stand upon, nor any thing to take hold of, there is nothing between you and hell but the air; it is only the power and mere pleasure of God that holds you up.

People clung to the pillars of the church, bracing themselves, fearing that at that very moment they were actually slipping into the fires of hell the preacher so vividly depicted. Many felt that if he would at any moment stop speaking, they would immediately drop into the doom and suffer the torments of the lost. Another minister sitting on the platform pulled at the preacher's coattails and yelled out, "Is not God also a God of mercy?"

The wrath of God burns against them, their damnation does not slumber; the pit is prepared, the fire is made ready, the furnace is now hot, ready to receive them; the flames do now rage and glow. The glittering sword is whet, and held over them, and the pit hath opened its mouth under them.

In almost every house throughout the town, people were crying out for God to save them. Hell became undeniably real and God became their only hope.

Thus all you that never passed under a great change of heart, by the mighty power of the Spirit of God upon your souls; all you that were never born again, and made new creatures, and raised from being dead in sin, to a state of new ... are in the hands of an angry God.

That night, Sunday, July 8, 1741, marked one of the pinnacle dates in the First Great Awakening. The preacher: Jonathan Edwards. The message: "Sinners in the Hands of an Angry God," arguably the most well-known sermon ever preached in American history.

Watch It!

Use the following space to take notes as you view the video in which Lee Strobel interviews Dr. Jerry Walls, professor of philosophy at Asbury Seminary in Wilmore, Kentucky, and author of the book *Hell: The Logic of Damnation*, and Gary Amirault, the founder of Tent Maker Ministries.

Discuss It!

1 Is the concept of hell relevant today? Why or why not? What do you think most people today believe about hell?

2 What do *you* believe concerning the concept of hell? On what basis have you come to your conclusions about hell? Which sources influenced your opinion about hell?

> "Go to heaven for the climate, hell for the company."
>
> **Mark Twain**

3 To what extent are the biblical depictions of hell as fiery images of eternal suffering intended to be taken literally or figuratively? If they're to be taken figuratively, what's the lesson they're trying to teach? How would you describe what hell is really like?

Are the Flames Literal?

Though many Christians believe the flames of hell are literal, others are convinced the Bible uses that imagery in a figurative way. Philosopher J. P. Moreland, for example, said: "We know that the reference to flames is figurative because if you try to take it literally, it makes no sense. For example, hell is described as a place of utter darkness and yet there are flames too. How can that be? Flames would light things up.

"In addition, we're told Christ is going to return surrounded by flames and that he's going to have a big sword coming out of his mouth. But nobody thinks Christ won't be able to say anything because he'll be choking on a sword. The figure of the sword stands for the word of God in judgment. The flames stand for Christ coming in judgment."

But whether literal or figurative, the reference to flames is meant to send an important message. "Any figure of speech has a literal point," Moreland said. "What is figurative is the burning flame; what is literal is that this is a place of utter heartbreak. It is a loss of everything, and it's meant to stand for the fact that hell is the worst possible situation that could ever happen to a person."

"I can hardly see how anyone ought to wish Christianity to be true: for if so the plain language of the text seems to show that the men who do not believe—and this would include my father, brother, and almost all of my best friends—will be everlastingly punished. And this is a damnable doctrine."

Charles Darwin

> "Now, if anything at all can be known to be wrong, it seems to me to be unshakably certain that it would be wrong to make any sentient being suffer eternally for any offense whatever."
>
> **Antony Flew,** *God, Freedom, and Immortality*

4 What are some common objections people have about the concept of hell?

5 If God is loving, what are some reasons why he would allow a place like hell to exist?

> "We must picture Hell as a state where everyone is perpetually concerned about his own dignity and advancement, where everyone has a grievance, and where everyone lives the deadly serious passions of envy, self-importance, and resentment."
>
> **C. S. Lewis**

6 Jerry Walls defines hell as a place for people who reject the only God that exists. He says, "If you reject the only God that exists, you reject happiness. Misery is inevitable." Give reasons why you might agree or disagree with this position.

Watch It!

Use the following space to take notes as Lee Strobel continues to interview Dr. Jerry Walls and Gary Amirault.

Discuss It!

7 Gary Amirault and Jerry Walls both agree that true happiness is a relationship with God through Jesus. But Amirault believes that *all* people will wind up in heaven because "in the end, all people will be restored back to God through Jesus Christ." What reasons make this position appealing to you? Do you agree with Amirault's thinking? Why or why not?

> "Abandon hope all ye that enter here."
> **Inscription above the entrance to hell in Dante's *Inferno***

8 Amirault reasons that because God forgives everyone, his forgiveness must be big enough to cover even someone like Adolf Hitler. What's your reaction to Amirault's conclusion? Where do you think Hitler is right now? Do you think that God overcame Hitler with love and took him to heaven, as Amirault claims? Why or why not?

"God is not merely a doddering old grandfather with a white beard who sits on a throne in the sky and smiles as he lets everyone pass by. He's not hanging around saying, 'Well, Hitler, you murdered a few folks at Dachau, Buchenwald and Auschwitz, but I understand you're simply a product of your environment. I'm all-forgiving; enter heaven.' That's not being loving—that's amoral. Instead of asking, 'How could a caring God allow a hell to exist?' the question ought to be, 'How could a caring God not allow a hell to exist?'"

Cliffe Knechtle, *Give Me an Answer*

9 Jerry Walls argues that forgiveness is a two-way street. He states, "I believe God loves the people in hell, but they don't love him back. And if they don't love God back they cannot experience heaven." Do you agree or disagree with Walls' reasoning? Explain your response.

10 Amirault claims, "I have yet to meet a person who rejects God's love. I *have* met people who reject Christians who preach a 'turn or burn' gospel. But people are born to receive God's love. We can't reject it." What's your reaction to this counterargument? What are some possible objections to the idea that all people wind up in heaven?

11 Can hell, God's justice, and God's love all be real and true at the same time? Or is God a failure, as Amirault asserts, if he can't save the whole world from hell? Explain.

12 Some theologians conclude from Jesus' teaching in Matthew 11:20–24 that everyone will not have the same experience in hell, but that there will be degrees of separation, isolation, and emptiness. In other words, justice will be adjusted according to the culpability of each individual. Does this influence your perception of the fairness of hell? How so?

"If every Christian could spend one minute in the fires of hell, he would become a soul winner the rest of his life and seek to warn men and women of the terrible and tragic fate that awaits those who believe not the gospel."

William Booth, founder, Salvation Army

13 According to the Bible verses listed below, what does the Bible teach about heaven (connection with God) and hell (separation from God)?

"Do not be afraid of those who kill the body but cannot kill the soul. Rather, be afraid of the One who can destroy both soul and body in hell." (Matthew 10:28)

If anyone's name was not found written in the book of life, he was thrown into the lake of fire. (Revelation 20:15)

But the cowardly, the unbelieving, the vile, the murderers, the sexually immoral, those who practice magic arts, the idolaters and all liars — their place will be in the fiery lake of burning sulfur. This is the second death. (Revelation 21:8)

"The Son of Man will send out his angels, and they will weed out of his kingdom everything that causes sin and all who do evil. They will throw them into the fiery furnace, where there will be weeping and gnashing of teeth." (Matthew 13:41 – 42; also Luke 16:19 – 31)

"Not everyone who says to me, 'Lord, Lord,' will enter the kingdom of heaven, but only he who does the will of my Father who is in heaven. Many will say to me on that day, 'Lord, Lord, did we not prophesy in your name, and in your name drive out demons and perform many miracles?' Then I will tell them plainly, 'I never knew you.'" (Matthew 7:21 – 23)

"God so loved the world that he gave his one and only Son, that whoever believes in him shall not perish but have eternal life. For God did not send his Son into the world to condemn the world, but to save the world through him. Whoever believes in him is not condemned, but whoever does not believe stands condemned already because he has not believed in the name of God's one and only Son." (John 3:16 – 18)

If you confess with your mouth, "Jesus is Lord," and believe in your heart that God raised him from the dead, you will be saved. For it is with your heart that you believe and are justified, and it is with your mouth that you confess and are saved. (Romans 10:9–10)

The Lord . . . is patient with you, not wanting anyone to perish, but everyone to come to repentance. (2 Peter 3:9)

14 Do you think that when people avoid or reject God and his involvement in their lives, they realize that they are actually choosing hell? On a more personal level, have *you* resisted God at times in your life? Explain.

Watch It! *Lee's Perspective*

The fairness of hell was a major stumbling block for me when I was a spiritual seeker. Ultimately, though, I saw enough of the justice behind eternal punishment that I didn't let the doctrine derail my spiritual journey. Especially helpful were the comments that theologian D. A. Carson made to me:

"Hell is not a place where people are consigned because they were pretty good blokes, but they just didn't believe the right stuff. They're consigned there, first and foremost, because they defy their maker and want to be at the center of the universe. Hell is not filled with people who have already repented, only God isn't gentle enough or good enough to let them out. It's filled with people who, for all eternity, still want to be the center of the universe and who persist in their God-defying rebellion.

"What is God to do? If he says it doesn't matter to him, then God is no longer a God to be admired. He's either amoral or positively creepy. For him to act in any other way in the face of such blatant defiance would be to reduce God himself."

Chart It!

At this point in your spiritual journey, what do you believe about hell? On a scale from one to ten, place an X near the spot and phrase that best describes you. Share your selection with the rest of the group and give reasons for placing your X where you did.

1	2	3	4	5	6	7	8	9	10
I'm not convinced hell exists.				I'm unsure what to believe about hell.				I'm convinced hell exists.	

Study It!

Take some time later this week to check out what the Bible teaches about the eternal destiny of those who accept God and those who reject him.

- ✦ Matthew 13:40–43
- ✦ Matthew 25:31–46
- ✦ Luke 16:19–31
- ✦ John 3:16
- ✦ Romans 1–3
- ✦ Romans 6:23
- ✦ 1 Corinthians 1:18–19

SESSION
4

Does Science
Point toward
a Creator?

Read It!

No Evidence?

"For those who believe in God, no explanation is necessary. For those who do not, no explanation is possible."

Opening lines of the film *The Song of Bernadette*

"I don't know if God exists, but it would be better for his reputation if he didn't."

Jules Renard, French writer

"If God did not exist it would be necessary to invent him."

Voltaire

"There cannot be a God because if there were one, I could not believe that I was not he."

Friedrich Nietzsche

"People see God every day, they just don't recognize him."

Pearl Bailey

"I cannot imagine how the clockwork of the universe can exist without a clockmaker."

Voltaire

"I'd have to say that the biggest reason why I don't believe in god is because there is no proof of his existence. Throughout the millions of years that man has been on earth, there has never been any solid evidence that there is a creator. If there is a god, wouldn't he want as many followers as possible? Why leave any doubt? Why not come to earth and tell everyone he exists? Or, better yet, make it so that everyone knows he is there."

Norm, in an online discussion

"Those who turn to God for comfort may find comfort but I do not think they will find God."

Mignon McLaughlin, *The Neurotic's Notebook*

"My studies in Speculative philosophy, metaphysics, and science are all summed up in the image of a mouse called man running in and out of every hole in the Cosmos hunting for the Absolute Cheese."

Benjamin De Casseres, American poet, 1873 – 1945

"I do not believe in a personal God and I have never denied this but have expressed it clearly. If something is in me which can be called religious then it is the unbounded admiration for the structure of the world so far as our science can reveal it."

Albert Einstein in a letter dated March 24, 1954

"I didn't see any God out there."

Yuri Gagarin, Soviet cosmonaut, after orbiting Earth

"God doesn't exist. Only silly, ignorant old women believe in him."

Ukrainian schoolteacher

"All I have seen teaches me to trust the Creator for all I have not seen."

Ralph Waldo Emerson

"I do not feel obliged to believe that the same God who has endowed us with sense, reason, and intellect has intended us to forgo their use."

Galileo

"The probability of life originating from accident is comparable to the probability of the unabridged dictionary resulting from an explosion in a printing factory."

Professor Edwin Conklin, Princeton University biologist

"Although science may solve the problem of how the universe began, it cannot answer the question: why does the universe bother to exist? I don't know the answer to that."

Stephen Hawking

"Ironically, the picture of the universe bequeathed to us by the most advanced twentieth-century science is closer in spirit to the vision presented in the Book of Genesis than anything offered by science since Copernicus."

Dr. Patrick Glynn, atheist-turned-Christian

"Proof is only applicable to very rarefied areas of philosophy and mathematics.... For the most part we are driven to acting on good evidence, without the luxury of proof. There is good evidence of the link between cause and effect. There is good evidence that the sun will rise tomorrow. There is good reason to believe that I am the same man as I was ten years ago. There is good reason to believe my mother loves me and is not just fattening me up for the moment when she will pop arsenic into my tea. And there is good reason to believe in God. Very good reason. Not conclusive proof, but very good reason just the same.... I believe it is much harder to reject the existence of a supreme being than accept it."

Michael Green, *Faith for the Non-Religious*

"God, were he all-powerful and perfectly good, would have created a world in which there was no unnecessary evil.... It has been contended that there is evil in this world—unnecessary evil—and that the more popular and philosophically more significant of the many attempts to explain this evil are completely unsatisfactory. Hence we must conclude from the existence of evil that there cannot be an omnipotent, benevolent God."

J. McCloskey, *God and Evil*

"Our personal concept of God—when we pray, for instance—is *worthless* unless it coincides with his revelation of himself."

Paul E. Little, *Know What You Believe*

"Religion is something left over from the infancy of our intelligence; it will fade away as we adopt reason and science as our guidelines."

Bertrand Russell

"God gave us ... two powerful and well-matched abilities: to prove things we find hard to believe and to believe in things we find hard to prove."

Michael Guillen, *Can a Smart Person Believe in God?*

"Question boldly even the existence of God."

Thomas Jefferson

"The best data we have (concerning the origin of the universe) are exactly what I would have predicted, had I nothing to go on but the five books of Moses, the Psalms, and the Bible as a whole."

Nobel Prize–winning physicist Arno Penzias

"The whole point of faith is to believe regardless of the evidence, which is the very antithesis of science."

Michael Shermer, publisher, *Skeptic* **magazine**

"The exquisite order displayed by our scientific understanding of the physical world calls for the divine."

Dr. Vera Kistiakowski, former professor of physics at MIT

"Charles Darwin didn't want to murder God, as he once put it. But he did."

Time **magazine**

So what do *you* say? Does God exist or not? Some people believe with certainty that he does, while others believe with equal certainty that he doesn't. Many others live with ambivalence. With so many compelling and contradictory ideas out there, how does anyone really know *what* to believe?

Watch It!

Use the following space to take notes as you view the video in which Lee Strobel interviews Dr. Stephen Meyer, director of the Center for Science and Culture at Seattle's Discovery Institute and coauthor of *Darwinism, Design, and Public Education*, and Dr. Michael Shermer, publisher of *Skeptic* magazine and author of *The Science of Good and Evil*.

Discuss It!

1 Do you believe there is a God or some kind of Intelligent Designer behind the origin of the universe? Why or why not?

2 Growing up, what did you learn about evolution? Did that influence your beliefs about God? How so?

3 Which of the following arguments by Dr. Stephen Meyer do you think best or least supports the argument for an Intelligent Designer? Do you think these reasons are sufficient to support the intelligent design theory? Explain your answer.

❑ The universe had a beginning and therefore must have had a cause.

❑ The universe is so finely tuned that if it were different in infinitesimally minor ways, it would be impossible for life to exist.

❑ The high-tech information-processing "machinery" being discovered by biologists in the lowest forms of life is too intricate and complex to have happened by chance and must have originated from some form of intelligence.

❑ Nature can produce patterns but not information. All information—whether in a book, drawing, or computer

code—hasanintellgentsource.Therefore,thebiological
information in DNA, which uses a four-character chemical alphabet to spell out the precise assembly instructions
for all the proteins out of which living things are built,
must have its roots in an intelligence.

4 Michael Shermer counters that the "default answer" to Meyer's points is *not* that there must be a designer, creator, or God
behind the universe, but rather, it is perfectly acceptable in science
to conclude "we don't know." Do you agree? Why or why not?

5 Shermer addresses Meyer's first point (that something that begins to exist needs a creator) by arguing that if God does not
need a creator, then the universe itself does not need a creator. Do
you agree or disagree with this line of reasoning? Explain.

"An atheist is a man who believes himself an accident."
Francis Thompson

6 Both Shermer and Meyer agree that the universe is designed, but one difference between them is how *well* it is designed. Shermer believes the universe is a tinkered patchwork, and not very well designed. Meyer disagrees and states that the universe is exquisitely designed. Who do you think is right? Give reasons for your response.

7 True or false: Everything that begins to exist *must* have a cause. True or false: Where there is design, there *must* be a designer. Give reasons for your answers.

"If there were no God, there would be no atheists."
G. K. Chesterton

8 Suppose, for a moment, that the intelligent design theory is correct. How would you answer Shermer's question, "Who created the intelligent creator?" Explain your response.

Watch It!

Use the following space to take notes as Lee Strobel continues to interview Dr. Stephen Meyer and Dr. Michael Shermer.

Discuss It!

9 Michael Shermer rules out the possibility of the supernatural at the outset. Two-time Nobel Prize–winner Linus Pauling said: "Science is the search for the truth." If Pauling is right, should scientists be free to consider the possibility of the supernatural if the evidence of cosmology, physics, and biochemistry point in that direction? Why or why not?

10 Stephen Meyer believes it's contradictory to say that God guides an inherently unguided natural process or that God designed a natural mechanism as a substitute for his design. Read the following Bible verses and other quotations. Do you think it is possible to believe in Darwinian evolution and still be a Christian? In other words, does Darwinism explain away the need for a Creator? Explain your answer.

> *By faith we understand that the universe was formed at God's command, so that what is seen was not made out of what was visible. (Hebrews 11:3)*

> *In the beginning God created the heavens and the earth. Now the earth was formless and empty, darkness was over the surface of the deep, and the Spirit of God was hovering over the waters. And God said, "Let there be light," and there was light. (Genesis 1:1 – 3)*

> *For since the creation of the world God's invisible qualities — his eternal power and divine nature — have been clearly seen, being understood from what has been made [that is, his creation], so that men are without excuse. (Romans 1:20)*

"By coupling undirected, purposeless variation to the blind, uncaring process of natural selection, Darwin made theological or spiritual explanations of life processes superfluous."

Evolutionary Biology

"[Darwin's] greatest accomplishment [was to show that] living beings can be explained as the result of a natural process, natural selection, without any need to resort to a Creator or other external agent."

Evolutionist Francisco Ayala

"A widespread theological view now exists saying that God started off the world, props it up and works through laws of nature, very subtly, so subtly that its action is undetectable. But that kind of God is effectively no different to my mind than atheism."

Evolutionist William Provine

"The whole point of Darwinism is to show that there is no need for a supernatural creator, because natural can do the creating by itself."

Phillip Johnson, author, *Darwin on Trial*

"You can have God *or* natural selection, but not both.... If we admit God into the process, Darwin argued, then God would ensure that only 'the right variations occurred ... and natural selection would be superfluous.'"

Nancy Pearcey

"I do not believe in God because I don't believe in Mother Goose."

Clarence Darrow

11 Do all scientists have motives? What are some examples? Are motives relevant in assessing the validity of scientific theories or can the data speak for themselves?

"Eighty-six percent of all Americans believe in God or a supreme being."

George **magazine**

12 To what extent do you think that science and Christianity are compatible? Explain.

13 Share some of the concrete reasons you have now for your belief—or disbelief—in the existence of God.

Watch It! *Lee's Perspective*

One of the main reasons I became an atheist was because of the theory of evolution I was taught in school. My conclusion was that if chemical evolution could explain the origin of life and if neo-Darwinism could explain its development and diversity, then God was clearly out of a job!

Ironically, though, even though my road to atheism was paved by science, so was my later journey to God. As I delved much deeper into the data, I found myself agreeing with hundreds of scientists—with doctorates from Cambridge, Stanford, Yale, Cornell, Rutgers, Chicago, Princeton, Cal-Berkeley, and other prestigious universities—who have publicly declared their skepticism over Darwin's grandest claims.

On the positive side, I learned that a series of scientific discoveries over the last fifty years in a wide range of disciplines—from cosmology, physics, and astronomy to biochemistry, genetics, and human consciousness—point powerfully and persuasively toward the existence of a Creator. I ended up writing a book, *The Case for a Creator*, to describe the evidence that I found the most convincing.

Ultimately, I found myself agreeing with Dr. James Tour, the noted nanoscientist from Rice University, who said: "Only a rookie who knows nothing about science would say science takes away from faith. If you really study science, it will bring you closer to God."

Chart It!

At this point in your spiritual journey, what do you believe about the existence of a Creator God? On a scale from one to ten, place an X near the spot and phrase that best describes you. Share your selection with the rest of the group and give reasons for placing your X where you did.

1	2	3	4	5	6	7	8	9	10
I'm not convinced that an Intelligent Designer created the universe.				I'm unsure what to believe on how the universe came into existence.				I'm convinced that God exists and that he created the universe.	

Study It!

Take some time later this week to check out what the Bible teaches about God's existence and how the universe came to be.

✦ Genesis 1
✦ Job 38–42
✦ Psalm 14:1
✦ Psalm 19:1–3
✦ Romans 1:18–32
✦ Hebrews 11:1–3

If you want to go deeper into the topics Lee introduced, get the complete story.

The Case for Christ
*A Journalist's Personal
Investigation of the
Evidence for Jesus*

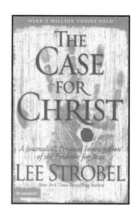

Is Jesus really the divine Son of God? What reason is there to believe that he is?

In his bestseller *The Case for Christ*, the legally trained investigative reporter Lee Strobel examined the claims of Christ by retracing his own spiritual journey, reaching the hard-won yet satisfying verdict that Jesus is God's unique son.

Written in the style of a blockbuster investigative report, *The Case for Christ* consults a dozen authorities on Jesus with doctorates from Cambridge, Princeton, Brandeis, and other topflight institutions to present:

- Historical evidence
- Scientific evidence
- Psychiatric evidence
- Fingerprint evidence
- Other evidence

This colorful, hard-hitting book is no novel. It's a riveting quest for the truth about history's most compelling figure.

"Lee Strobel asks the questions a tough-minded skeptic would ask. Every inquirer should have it."

> —*Phillip E. Johnson, law professor,
> University of California at Berkeley*

Hardcover 0-310-22646-5
Softcover 0-310-20930-7
Evangelism Pack 0-310-22605-8
Mass Market 6-pack 0-310-22627-9
Audio Pages® Abridged Cassette 0-310-24824-8
Audio Pages® Unabridged Cassette 0-310-21960-4
Audio Pages® Unabridged CD 0-310-24779-9

The Case for Faith

A Journalist Investigates the Toughest Objections to Christianity

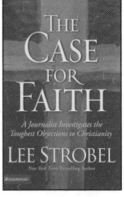

In his best-seller *The Case for Christ*, Lee Strobel examined the claims of Christ, reaching the hard-won yet satisfying verdict that Jesus is God's unique son.

But despite the compelling historical evidence that Strobel presented, many grapple with doubts or serious concerns about faith in God. As in a court of law, they want to shout, "Objection!" They say, "If God is love, then what about all of the suffering that festers in our world?" Or, "If Jesus is the door to heaven, then what about the millions who have never heard of him?"

In *The Case for Faith*, Strobel turns his tenacious investigative skills to the most persistent emotional objections to belief, the eight "heart" barriers to faith. *The Case for Faith* is for those who may be feeling attracted toward Jesus, but who are faced with formidable intellectual barriers standing squarely in their path. For Christians, it will deepen their convictions and give them fresh confidence in discussing Christianity with even their most skeptical friends.

Hardcover 0-310-22015-7
Softcover 0-310-23469-7
Evangelism Pack 0-310-23508-1
Mass Market 6-pack 0-310-23509X
Audio Pages® Abridged Cassettes 0-310-23475-1

Pick up a copy today at your favorite bookstore!

GRAND RAPIDS, MICHIGAN 49530 USA

WWW.ZONDERVAN.COM

> *"My road to atheism was paved by science . . . . But, ironically, so was my later journey to God."*—Lee Strobel

The Case for a Creator:
A Journalist Investigates Scientific Evidence That Points Toward God

Lee Strobel, Author of
The Case for Christ *and*
The Case for Faith

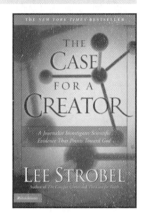

During his academic years, Lee Strobel became convinced that God was outmoded, a belief that colored his ensuing career as an award-winning journalist at the *Chicago Tribune*. Science had made the idea of a Creator irrelevant—or so Strobel thought.

But today science is pointing in a different direction. In recent years, a diverse and impressive body of research has increasingly supported the conclusion that the universe was intelligently designed. At the same time, Darwinism has faltered in the face of concrete facts and hard reason.

Has science discovered God? At the very least, it's giving faith an immense boost as new findings emerge about the incredible complexity of our universe. Join Strobel as he reexamines the theories that once led him away from God. Through his compelling and highly readable account, you'll encounter the mind-stretching discoveries from cosmology, cellular biology, DNA research, astronomy, physics, and human consciousness that present astonishing evidence in *The Case for a Creator*.

Hardcover: 0-310-24144-8
Unabridged Audio Pages® CD: 0-310-25439-6

ebooks:
Adobe Acrobat eBook Reader®: 0-310-25977-0
Microsoft Reader®: 0-310-25978-9
Palm™ Edition: 0-310-25979-7
Unabridged ebook Download: 0-310-26142-2

The Case for Easter
A Journalist Investigates the Evidence for the Resurrection

Lee Strobel

Did Jesus of Nazareth really rise from the dead?

Of the many world religions, only one claims that its founder returned from the grave. The resurrection of Jesus Christ is the very cornerstone of Christianity.

But a dead man coming back to life? In our sophisticated age, when myth has given way to science, who can take such a claim seriously? Some argue that Jesus never died on the cross. Conflicting accounts make the empty tomb seem suspect. And post-crucifixion sightings of Jesus have been explained in psychological terms.

How credible is the evidence for—and against—the resurrection? Focusing his award-winning skills as a legal journalist on history's most compelling enigma, Lee Strobel retraces the startling findings that led him from atheism to belief. Drawing on expert testimony first shared in his blockbuster book *The Case for Christ,* Strobel examines:

The Medical Evidence—Was Jesus' death a sham and his resurrection a hoax?

The Evidence of the Missing Body—Was Jesus' body really absent from his tomb?

The Evidence of Appearances—Was Jesus seen alive after his death on the cross?

Written in a hard-hitting journalistic style, *The Case for Easter* probes the core issues of the resurrection. Jesus Christ, risen from the dead: superstitious myth or life-changing reality? The evidence is in. The verdict is up to you.

Mass Market: 0-310-25475-2

The Case for Christmas
A Journalist Investigates the Identity of the Child in the Manger

Lee Strobel

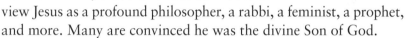

Who was in the manger that first Christmas morning?

Some say he would become a great moral leader. Others, a social critic. Still others view Jesus as a profound philosopher, a rabbi, a feminist, a prophet, and more. Many are convinced he was the divine Son of God.

Who was he — really? And how can you know for sure?

Consulting experts on the Bible, archaeology, and messianic prophecy, Lee Strobel searches out the true identity of the child in the manger. Join him as he asks the tough, pointed questions you'd expect from an award-winning legal journalist. If Jesus really was God in the flesh, then there ought to be credible evidence, including

Eyewitness Evidence — Can the biographies of Jesus be trusted?

Scientific Evidence — What does archaeology reveal?

Profile Evidence — Did Jesus fulfill the attributes of God?

Fingerprint Evidence — Did Jesus uniquely match the identity of the Messiah?

The Case for Christmas invites you to consider why Christmas matters in the first place. Somewhere beyond the traditions of the holiday lies the truth. It may be more compelling than you've realized. Weigh the facts ... and decide for yourself.

Jacketed Hardcover: 0-310-26629-7

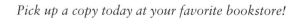

The Case for Faith
Visual Edition

Lee Strobel

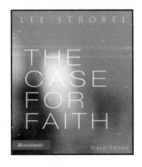

Open this book and open your eyes. It is unlike any other you have held; a visual feast for your eyes and a spiritual feast for your soul. Lee Strobel, former atheist and award-winning legal editor of the *Chicago Tribune*, asks hard questions about God in *The Case for Faith* Visual Edition. And then he explores them with evidence from archaeology, history, and science—all set in powerful imagery and stunning typography. See the evidence for faith as you've never seen it before.

Softcover: 0-310-25906-1

Pick up a copy today at your favorite bookstore!

ZONDERVAN™

GRAND RAPIDS, MICHIGAN 49530 USA

WWW.ZONDERVAN.COM

God's Outrageous Claims
Discover What They Mean for You

Lee Strobel

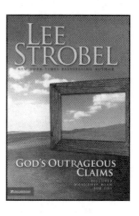

Lee Strobel presents thirteen phenomenal claims by God that can change the entire trajectory of your life and revolutionize your attitude, your character, and your relationships.

Take the Bible seriously and you'll discover that God makes some pretty amazing claims about you—and about what he wants to do in your life. *God's Outrageous Claims* examines important assertions that can transform your life into an adventure of faith, growth, and lasting fulfillment.

Discover how to grow in virtue, relate to others with authenticity, and make a real difference. *God's Outrageous Claims* is your guide to an exciting and challenging spiritual journey that can change you and your world profoundly.

Jacketed Hardcover: 0-310-26612-2

Pick up a copy today at your favorite bookstore!

ZONDERVAN™

GRAND RAPIDS, MICHIGAN 49530 USA

WWW.ZONDERVAN.COM

Tough Questions

Garry Poole and Judson Poling

"The profound insights and candor captured in these guides
will sharpen your mind, soften your heart, and inspire you and
the members of your group to find vital answers together."

—Bill Hybels

This second edition of Tough Questions, designed for use in any
small group setting, is ideal for use in seeker small groups. Based
on more than five years of field-tested feedback, extensive revi-
sions make this best-selling series easier to use and more appealing
than ever for both participants and group leaders.

Softcover

How Does Anyone Know God Exists? ISBN 0-310-24502-8

What Difference Does Jesus Make? ISBN 0-310-24503-6

How Reliable Is the Bible? ISBN 0-310-24504-4

How Could God Allow Suffering and Evil? ISBN 0-310-24505-2

Don't All Religions Lead to God? ISBN 0-310-24506-0

Do Science and the Bible Conflict? ISBN 0-310-24507-9

Why Become a Christian? ISBN 0-310-24508-7

Leader's Guide ISBN 0-310-24509-5

THE COMPLETE BOOK OF QUESTIONS

Garry Poole

Everyone has a story to tell or an opinion to share. *The Complete Book of Questions* helps you get the conversational ball rolling. Created especially for seeker small groups, these questions can jumpstart any conversation. They invite people to open up about themselves and divulge their thoughts, and provide the spark for stimulating discussions. This generous compilation of questions can be used in just about any context to launch great conversations.

Questions cover ten thematic categories, from light and easy questions such as "What room in your house best reflects your personality?" to deeper, more spiritual questions such as, "If God decided to visit the planet right now, what do you think he would do?" *The Complete Book of Questions* is a resource that can help small group leaders draw participants out and couples, friends, and families get to know one another better.

Softcover: ISBN 0-310-24420-X

We want to hear from you. Please send your comments about this
book to us in care of zreview@zondervan.com. Thank you.

GRAND RAPIDS, MICHIGAN 49530 USA

ZONDERVAN.COM/
AUTHORTRACKER